GOD IS THE GARDENER

and

PROFILE OF A PROPHET

GOD IS THE GARDENER

and

PROFILE OF A PROPHET

Hugh B. Brown

CLASSIC TALK SERIES

Deseret Book Company
Salt Lake City, Utah

Reprinted with permission.

Library of Congress Catalog Card Number: 97-78183

ISBN 0-87579-974-4

Printed in the United States of America   72082-4585C

10   9   8   7   6   5   4   3   2

GOD IS THE GARDENER

I want to speak about humor for just a minute. Golden Kimball is reported to have said that "The Lord himself must like a joke or he wouldn't have made some of you people." I hope none of you will take that personally.

It is indeed a daring, if not a reckless venture, for an octogenarian to undertake to speak across a void of sixty years to a group of vibrant young students who are graduating. But knowing of your four years of training, especially in patience and endurance in your classes, I think you'll have some sympathy for me if I attempt to address you from the far side of the stream of life.

I should like to congratulate the graduating class and all the students of this great university on the fact that you have kept pretty much aloof from the activities that have been prevalent on the campuses of many other universities, where students have attempted to take control, not only of the disciplinary activities on the campus itself, but to supplant civil government, both on the campus and in life. It's too bad that these young people have thought to try to supersede established government. We cannot agree with their attempts to get what they want by means of force. I congratulate the members, too, of the student body and the faculty, on what President Wilkinson has referred to, namely, accepting the call to duty in our great land when it comes and not shirking the responsibility incident to that call.

There is another matter I want to speak of briefly. You young people are leaving your university at a time in which our nation is engaged in an abrasive and increasingly strident process of electing a president. I wonder if you would permit me, one who has managed to survive a number of these events, to pass on to you a few words of counsel. First, I'd like you to be reassured that the leaders of both major political parties in this land are men of integrity and unquestioned patriotism. Beware of those who feel obliged to prove their own patriotism by calling into question the loyalty of others. Be skeptical of those who attempt to demonstrate their love of country by demeaning its institutions. Know that men of both major political parties who guide the nation's executive, legislative, and judicial branches are men of unquestioned loyalty, and we should stand by and support them. And this refers not only to one party, but to all. Strive to develop a maturity of mind and emotion and a depth of spirit which will enable you to differ with others on matters of politics without calling into question the integrity of those with whom you differ. Allow within the bounds of your definition of religious orthodoxy a variation of political belief. Do not have the temerity to dogmatize on issues where the Lord has seen fit to be silent.

I have found by long experience that our two-party system is sound. Beware of those who are so lacking in humility that they cannot come within the framework of one of our two great parties. Our nation has avoided chaos like that which is gripping France today because men have been able to temper their own desires sufficiently to seek broad agreement within one of the two major parties, rather than forming splinter groups around one radical idea. Our two-party system has served us well and should not be lightly discarded. At a time when radicals of right or left would inflame race against race, avoid those who preach evil doctrines of racism. When our Father declared that we, his children, are brothers and sisters, he did not limit this relationship on the basis of race. Strive to develop that true love of country, which realizes that real patriotism must include within it a regard for the people, the inhabitants of the rest of the globe. Patriots have never demanded of good men the hatred of another country as proof of one's love for his own. Acquire tolerance and compassion for others and for those of a different political persuasion or race or religion. This is something demanded by the heavenly parentage which we all have in common.

Now I'd like to bring to your attention one of the oldest subjects known to man, timeless in interest, always up-to-date, and imperative in its appeal. It is a subject on which the Savior spent much time, one with which philosophers have wrestled and on which scientists have ventured great, learned, and thoughtful opinions. From the beginning of time right down to this space and atomic age, this has been a lively subject, imperative in its demands. It is a topic vitally important to each and all of us from the time we enter this world until we leave it, and then on throughout eternity. The subject I wish to discuss, briefly but reverently, is God and man's relationship to Him.

In the tenth chapter of Luke we read, "Thou shalt love the Lord thy God with all thy heart, and with all thy soul, and with all thy strength, and with all thy mind" (v. 27). Can a man love God with his mind, or is the mind limited to those cold processes of reasoning only? You young men and women have already begun to study and to marvel at the wonders of your universe. Your maturing and inquiring minds have caused you to ask, "Who was in control when all this was set in motion?" I would rather you'd find a reverent and truthful answer to that question than to be able to read in Greek and Hebrew or to read the planet's or nature's story in stone and earth and plant. In other words, I would have you put first things first and begin your education at the center of your heart. As these convictions grow, you will hunger and thirst after knowledge, even as a plant thirsts for water. You'll come to realize that all the knowledge which is obtainable in the best universities, without some underlying synthesis or some understandable meaning and purpose, without these it would be incomplete and wholly inadequate. I'm pleading for you to take note of the underlying truths having to do with our universe, with our lives, and with our purpose in life, and then to live as though we believe what we say when we say we believe in God. Jesus said that if you'd have life eternal, you must know God. As we progressively come to know him, we'll be prompted to emulate him, and that's the thing I'd like to leave with this graduating class and call to the attention of all of us—that as we progressively come to know God, we will undeniably and constantly be reminded of the possibility of our emulating him and thereby becoming more like him.

I was in Colorado Springs recently. A guest of the Air Force Academy and a speaker to the cadets, I was taken by the commanding officer on a tour of the facility and the campus there. We came to a wonderful monument, topped by a falcon with spreading wings. On the base of this monument I read these words, "Man's flight through life is sustained by the power of his knowledge." And I asked myself the question,

"What knowledge? Which phase of knowledge, which branch of learning, will most definitely and inspiringly take care of man's flight through life?" I concluded that man's life and his flight through life are sustained most by a knowledge of God and of man. I submit to you that faith in a personal God, one who can be referred to as Father, gives one a sense of dignity and holds before one an ideal toward which to strive. He is real, as you and I are real. And I want to impress that on the minds of you young students as you go out into the world—that you have someone greater than yourself dwelling with you and on whom you can call.

In the story of the Creation, these words are recorded in Genesis, "So God created man in his own image, in the image of God created he him; male and female created he them" (Genesis 1:27). It was doubtless this thought of man being in God's image, in a godlike status, that prompted the Apostle John to say, "Now are we the sons of God, and it doth not yet appear what we shall be: but we know that, when he shall appear, we shall be like him; for we shall see him as he is" (1 John 3:2). Across the centuries, no experience has been more universal and helpful in the sense of someone caring for us, near enough to be called upon, responsive enough to understand. He is real and he is personal and should be idealized but also realized. We must not only possess the idea of God, but we should be possessed by it. Men do not believe in God because they have proved him. Rather they try endlessly to prove him because they can't help believing in him. He has established that in the hearts of his children.

You are now alumni, not only of a Church-related institution, but one which is Church-owned and operated. Be grateful for that fact, young people. As you consider the history of education in America, you may be surprised by what religion has done to the great universities of our land and of the world. I am indebted to Reverend Earl L. Riley of the First Baptist Church of Salt Lake City, for some statistical information, which I would like to share with you. "Pericles founded his civilization upon common culture, and it failed. Caesar founded his civilization upon law, and it failed. Alexander founded his civilization upon power, and it also failed. But our forefathers knew that any other basis than religion and education, the two greatest forces in the world, would be inadequate as a basis upon which to build a civilization, and that if it were built upon anything less than real religion and good education, we'd have only an artificial structure. Twenty-three of the first twenty-four universities built in America were built by religious organizations. Out of a hundred and nineteen educational institutions, east of the Mississippi, a hundred and three of them were built by religious organizations. For the first hundred and fifty years in America, churches provided all the institutions of higher learning. From these halls came leaders of thought and champions of liberty who made our republic possible. Jefferson was an alumnus of William and Mary. James Madison of Princeton. Alexander Hamilton was an alumnus of what is now the Columbia University. It is interesting to note that all but eight of the fifty-five who signed the Declaration of Independence, and most of those who wrote the Constitution, breathed the atmosphere of church-supported institutions of learning. Thomas Jefferson declared that people cannot be ignorant and free. Founding of the University of Virginia was the crowning achievement of his life. Benjamin Franklin rejoiced that he was the founder of the University of Pennsylvania.

George Washington left a fifty-thousand dollar bequest, and Washington and Lee University was the recipient of the legacy. The early leaders of church and state in America were the products of schools begun by orthodox Christianity. Sixteen of the first eighteen presidents were college graduates from church-related institutions of higher learning. Seven of the first Chief Justices of the Supreme Court were college graduates, graduating from church-related schools."

Now you have been taught, young people, to believe that God and man belong to a society of eternal intelligences. Differences exist, of course, indescribably great, but more of degree rather than of kind. The idea of a supreme being is indelibly stamped on the inner-consciousness of men. Though man is to some extent master of his destiny, he is conscious of the supreme source of his existence. Dr. James E. Talmage sums up the discussion of creation and the

universe as follows: "What is man in this bound-
less setting of sublime splendor? I answer you,
potentially now, but actually to be, man is
greater and grander, more precious in the arith-
metic of God than all the planets and suns of
space. For him they were created." I'm reading
this because I'd like you to feel the dignity of
man. And dignify it by your conduct as you go
forward as responsible citizens of our country
and representatives of this great university. In
this world, man is given dominion over a few
things; it is his privilege to achieve supremacy
over many things. The heavens declare the glory
of God, and the firmament showeth his handi-
work, incomprehensibly grand as are the physi-
cal creations of the earth and space. They have
been brought into existence as a means to an
end, necessary to the realization of the supreme
purpose, which in the words of the Creator is
thus declared, "Behold, this is my work and my

glory—to bring to pass the immortality and eternal life of man" (Moses 1:39).

Some theologians tell us that God is incomprehensible. But He says that to know Him is life eternal. The one view takes hope out of life, the other is an eternal beacon. Sometimes young people say we older ones are behind the times, and they're probably right. They're certainly right. But, during the time that is behind me— and I bring this to you as a testimony—during the time that is behind me, I have developed a faith in a personal, living God, which I consider to be the most priceless possession. It has been my glorious privilege, progressively, to know Him. Such faith gives order, meaning, stimulus, and direction to life. We cannot know him by the intellect alone nor with bodily senses alone nor by only reading scripture, but by inspiration, the illumination of the soul, such as was experienced by Peter when he replied to the question of Christ, "Whom say ye that I am?" And he said, without hesitation, though it was a surprise to him what he said, "Thou art the Christ, the Son of the Living God." And Christ replied to him, "Flesh and blood hath not revealed it unto thee, but my Father which is in Heaven" (Matthew 16:15–17). If you'll always keep in mind that you are actually the children of your Heavenly Father, that there is something of him in you, that you may aspire to become something like that from which you came, and to cooperate with him in the unfinished work of creation, you will remember that his plan for the salvation of his children has purpose behind it—a design to be carried out. If you keep these great truths in mind, you'll be fortified and sustained, whatever life may hold for you.

It is important not only that you keep growing, but that you be versatile, adaptive, and unafraid to venture. In other words, be up-to-date. Seek to obtain a certain flexibility of mind, which will inspire you to listen, to learn, and to adapt as you move forward into a new and ever expanding universe. Of the cowardice that shrinks from new truths, someone has said, "From the laziness that is content with half-truth, from the arrogance that thinks it knows all the truth, Oh, God of Truth, deliver us!" In the process of self-discovery you will sometimes stand amazed at what you've progressively become aware of, having to do with your potential range and your abilities. You will not then be discouraged by a failure or two along the way, as long as you are learning and growing. I leave with you my humble testimony in respect to these things.

Now some of you as you go forward are going to meet with disappointment, perhaps many disappointments, some of them crucial. Sometimes you will wonder whether God has forgotten you. Sometimes you may even wonder if he lives and where he has gone. But in these times when so many are saying God is dead, and where so many are denying his existence, I think I could not leave with you a better message than this: God is aware of you individually. He knows who you are and what you are, and, furthermore, he knows what you are capable of becoming. Be not discouraged then, if you do not get all the things you want just when you want them. Have the courage to go on and face your life and if necessary reverse it to bring it into harmony with his law.

Could I tell you just a quick story out of my own experience in life? Sixty odd years ago, I was on a farm in Canada. I had purchased the farm from another who had been somewhat careless in keeping it up, and I went out one morning and found a currant bush, at least six feet high. I knew that it was going all to wood, there was no sign of blossom or of fruit. I had

had some experience in pruning trees before we left Salt Lake to go to Canada, as my father had a fruit farm. So I got my pruning shears and went to work on the currant bush, and I clipped it and cut it and cut it down until there was nothing left but a little clump of stumps. And as I looked at them, I yielded to an impulse, which I often have, to talk with inanimate things and have them talk to me. It's a ridiculous habit, one I can't overcome. As I looked at this little clump of bushes, stumps, there seemed to be a tear on each one, and I said, "What's the matter currant bush? What are you crying about?" And I thought I heard that currant bush speak. It seemed to say, "How could you do this to me? I was making such wonderful growth. I was almost as large as the fruit tree and the shade tree, and now you've cut me down. And all in the garden will look upon me with contempt and pity. How could you do it? I thought you were the gardener here." I thought I heard that from the currant bush. I thought it so much that I answered it. I said, "Look, little currant bush, I *am* the gardener here, and I know what I want you to be. If I let you go the way you want to go, you'll never amount to anything. But, someday, when you are ladened with fruit, you're going to think back and say, 'Thank you, Mr. Gardener, for cutting me down, for loving me enough to hurt me.'"

Ten years passed, and I found myself in Europe. I had made some progress in the First World War in the Canadian Army. In fact I was a field officer, and there was only one man between me and the rank of general, which I had cherished in my heart for years. Then he became a casualty. And the day after, I received a telegram from London. General Turner, in charge of all Canadian officers, said, "Be in my office tomorrow morning at ten o'clock."

I puffed up. I called my special servant. (We called them "Batmen" over there.) I said, "Polish my boots and my buttons. Make me look like a general because I'm going up tomorrow to be appointed." He did the best he could with what he had to work on, and I went to London.

I walked into the office of the general. I saluted him smartly, and he replied to my salute, as higher officers usually do to juniors: sort of a "Get out of the way, worm." Then he said, "Sit down, Brown." I was deflated. I sat down. And he said, "Brown, you're entitled to this promotion, but I cannot make it. You've qualified, passed the regulations, you've had the experience, you're entitled to it in every way, but I cannot make this appointment." Just then he went into the other room to answer a phone call, and I did what most every officer and man in the army would do under those circumstances: I looked over on his desk to see what my personal history sheet showed. And I saw written on the bottom of that history sheet in large, capital letters, "THIS MAN IS A MORMON."

Now at that time, we were hated heartily in Britain, and I knew why he couldn't make the appointment. Finally he came back and said, "That's all, Brown." I saluted him, less heartily than before, and went out. On my way back to Shorencliff, a hundred and twenty miles away, I thought every turn of the wheel that clacked across the rails was saying, "You're a failure. You must go home and be called a coward by those who do not understand." And bitterness rose in my heart until when I arrived, finally, in my tent, I rather vigorously threw my cap on the cot, together with my Sam Brown belt. I clenched my fist, and I shook it at heaven, and I said, "How could you do this to me, God? I've done everything that I knew how to do to uphold the standards of the Church. I was making such wonderful growth and now you've cut me down. How could you do it?"

And then I heard a voice. It sounded like my own voice, and the voice said, "I'm the gardener here, I know what I want you to be. If I let you go the way you want to go, you'll never amount to anything. And, someday, when you are ripened in life, you're going to shout back across the time, and say, 'Thank you, Mr. Gardener, for cutting me down, for loving me enough to hurt me.'"

But those words, which I recognize now as my words to the currant bush, which had become God's word to me, drove me to my knees, where I prayed for forgiveness for my arrogance and my ambition.

As I was praying there I heard some Mormon boys in an adjoining tent singing the closing number to an M.I.A. session, which I usually attended with them. And I recognized these words, which all of you have memorized: "It may not be on the mountain height Or over the stormy sea, It may not be at the battle's front My Lord will have need of me. . . . So trusting my all to thy tender care, And knowing thou lovest me, I'll do thy will with a heart sincere, I'll be what you want me to be."

My young friends and brothers and sisters, will you remember that little experience, which changed my whole life? Had the Gardener not taken control and done for me what was best for me, or if I had gone the way I wanted to go, I would have returned to Canada as a senior commanding officer of Western Canada. I would have raised my family in a barracks. My six daughters would have had little chance to marry in the Church. I myself would probably have gone down and down, I do not know what might have happened. But this I know, and this I say to you and to Him in your presence, looking back over sixty years, "Thank you, Mr. Gardener, for cutting me down."

Now I leave with you my testimony, and I received this testimony from the same source which Jesus said inspired Peter, when the chief Apostle said, "Thou art the Christ!" Whatever undertakings may demand of you and your attention, I tell you, young men, young women, you cannot make a better resolution today than this: "I am going to keep close to the Lord. I am going to understand him better, and understanding him, I will understand myself and will try to put my life into harmony with his." For I have come to know that every man, every woman, has potential godhood dwelling in him, for God is in reality the father of us all. I leave you my blessing: God bless these young people. They're looking forward hopefully and gleefully to the experiences of life. Oh, Father, be with and sustain them, uphold them, deepen their testimonies, keep them true to the faith and true to themselves. Father, bless them that they may live up to the best traditions of our country and be proud of the fact that they graduated from a Church owned and operated school where they were taught these precious truths concerning the purpose of their life and their relationship to Deity, I pray in the name of Jesus Christ, amen.

From a transcript of an address given at Brigham Young University at the Ninety-Third Annual Commencement Exercises on 31 May 1968, while Elder Brown was serving as first counselor in the First Presidency.

PROFILE OF A PROPHET

I should like to dispense with all formality, if I may, and address both faculty and students as my brothers and sisters. I adopt that form of salutation for several reasons. First, that practically all who are here are members of the Church which established and maintains this university. Secondly, because I believe in the fatherhood of God and the brotherhood of man. Third, I do not intend to give a lecture, certainly not an oration or even a sermon, but simply wish to bear my testimony to my brothers and sisters.

I should like to be for a few minutes a witness in support of the proposition that the gospel of Jesus Christ has been restored in our day and that this is his Church, which was organized under his direction through the Prophet Joseph Smith. I should like to give some reasons for the faith I have and for my allegiance to the Church. Perhaps I can do this more quickly by referring to an interview I had in London, England, in 1939, just before the outbreak of the war. I had met a very prominent English gentleman, a member of the House of Commons, formerly one of the Justices of the Supreme Court of England. In my conversations with this gentleman, on various subjects, "vexations of the soul" he called them, we talked about business and law, about politics, international relations and war, and we frequently discussed religion. He called me on the phone one day and asked if I would meet him at his office and explain some phases of the gospel. He said, "I think there is going to be a war. If there is, you will have to return to America, and we may not meet again." His statement regarding the imminence of war and the possibility that we would not meet again proved to be prophetic. When I went to his office he said he was intrigued by some things I had told him. He asked me to prepare a brief of Mormonism.

I may say to you students that a brief is a statement of law and facts that lawyers such as President [Ernest L.] Wilkinson prepare when they are going into court to argue a case.

He asked me to prepare a brief on Mormonism and discuss it with him as I would discuss a legal problem. He said, "You have told me that you believe that Joseph Smith was a prophet. You have said to me that you believe that God the Father and Jesus of Nazareth appeared to Joseph Smith. I cannot understand how a barrister and solicitor from Canada, a man trained in logic and evidence could accept such absurd statements. What you tell me about Joseph Smith seems fantastic, but I think you should take three days at least to prepare a brief and permit me to examine it and question you on it.

I suggested that we proceed at once and have an Examination for Discovery, which is briefly a meeting of the opposing sides in a lawsuit where the plaintiff and defendant, with their attorneys, meet to examine each other's claims and see if they can find some area of agreement, thus saving the time of the court later on. I said perhaps we could see whether we had some common ground from which we could discuss my "fantastic ideas." He agreed to that quite readily.

I can only give you, in the few minutes at my disposal, a condensed and abbreviated synopsis of the three-hour conversation which followed. In the interest of time I shall resort to the question and answer method rather than narration. I began by asking, "May I proceed, sir, on the assumption that you are a Christian?"

"I am."

"I assume you believe in the Bible—the Old and New Testament?"

"I do!"

"Do you believe in prayer?"

"I do!"

"You say that my belief that God spoke to a man in this age is fantastic and absurd?"

"To me, it is."

"Do you believe that God ever did speak to anyone?"

"Certainly, all through the Bible we have evidence of that."

"Did he speak to Adam?"

"Yes."

"To Enoch, Noah, Abraham, Moses, Jacob, Joseph and on through the prophets?"

"I believe he spoke to each of them."

"Do you believe that contact between God and man ceased when Jesus appeared on the earth?"

"No, such communication reached its climax, its apex, at that time."

"Do you believe that Jesus was the Son of God?"

"He was."

"Do you believe, sir, that after Jesus was resurrected a certain lawyer, who was also a tentmaker by the name of Saul of Tarsus, when on his way to Damascus, talked with Jesus of Nazareth, who had been crucified, resurrected, and had ascended into heaven?"

"I do."

"Whose voice did Saul hear?"

"It was the voice of Jesus Christ, for he so introduced himself."

"Then, my Lord (that is the way we address judges in the British Commonwealth), my Lord, I am submitting to you in all seriousness that it was standard procedure in Bible times for God to talk to man."

"I think I will admit that, but it stopped shortly after the first century of the Christian era."

"Why do you think it stopped?"

"I can't say."

"You think that God hasn't spoken since then?"

"I am sure he hasn't."

"There must be a reason; can you give me a reason?"

"I do not know."

"May I suggest some possible reasons:

Perhaps God does not speak to man anymore because he cannot. He has lost the power."

He said, "Of course that would be blasphemous."

"Well, then, if you don't accept that, perhaps he doesn't speak to men because he doesn't love us anymore. He is no longer interested in the affairs of men."

"No," he said, "God loves all men, and he is no respecter of persons."

"Well, then, if he could speak, and if he loves us, then the only other possible answer as I see it is that we don't need him. We have made such rapid strides in science, we are so well-educated, that we don't need God anymore."

And then he said, and his voice trembled as he thought of impending war, "Mr. Brown, there never was a time in the history of the world when the voice of God was needed as it is needed now. Perhaps you can tell me why he doesn't speak."

My answer was, "He does speak; he has spoken, but men need faith to hear him."

Then we proceeded to prepare what I may call a "profile of a prophet."

Perhaps you students would like to amplify what I must condense today—draw your own standard or definition of a prophet and see whether Joseph Smith measures up.

We agreed, between us, that the following characteristics should distinguish a man who claims to be a prophet.

A. He will boldly claim that God has spoken to him.

B. Any man so claiming would be a dignified man with a dignified message; no table-jumping, no whisperings from the dead, no clairvoyance, but an intelligent statement of truth.

C. Any man claiming to be a prophet of God would declare his message without fear and without making any weak concessions to public opinion.

D. If he were speaking for God he could not make concessions although what he taught would be new and contrary to the accepted teachings of the day. A prophet bears witness to what he has seen and heard and seldom tries to make a case by argument. His message and not himself is important.

E. Such a man would speak in the name of the Lord, saying, "Thus saith the Lord," as did Moses, Joshua, and others.

F. Such a man would predict future events in the name of the Lord and they would come to pass, as did Isaiah and Ezekiel.

G. He would have not only an important message for his time, but often a message for all future time, such as Daniel, Jeremiah, and others had.

H. He would have courage and faith enough to endure persecution and to give his life, if need be, for the cause he espoused, such as Peter, James, Paul, and others did.

I. Such a man would denounce wickedness fearlessly. He would generally be rejected or persecuted by the people of his time, but later generations, the descendants of his persecutors, would build monuments in his honor.

J. He would be able to do superhuman things, things that no man could do without God's help. The consequence or result of his message and work would be convincing evidence of his prophetic calling: "By their fruits ye shall know them."

K. His teachings would be in strict conformity with scripture and his words and his writings would become scripture. "For the prophecy

came not in old time by the will of man: but holy
men of God spake as they were moved by the
Holy Ghost" (2 Peter 1:21).

Now, I have given but an outline which you
can fill in and amplify and then measure and
judge the Prophet Joseph Smith by the work and
stature of other prophets.

As a student of the life of the Prophet Joseph
Smith for more than fifty years, I say to you
young men and women, by these standards
Joseph Smith qualifies as a prophet of God.

I believe that Joseph Smith was a prophet of
God because he talked like a prophet. He was
the first man since the apostles of Jesus Christ
were slain to make the claim which prophets
have always made, namely, that God had spoken to him. He lived and died like a prophet. I
believe he was a prophet of God because he
gave to this world some of the greatest of all revelations. I believe that he was a prophet of God

because he predicted many things which have come to pass, things which only God could bring to pass.

John, the beloved disciple of Jesus, declared, "The testimony of Jesus is the spirit of prophecy" (Revelation 19:10). If Joseph Smith had the testimony of Jesus he had the spirit of prophecy, and if he had the spirit of prophecy he was a prophet. I submit to you, and I submitted to my friend, that as much as any man who ever lived, Joseph had a testimony of Jesus for, like the apostles of old, he saw him and heard him speak. He gave his life for that testimony. I challenge any man to name one who has given more evidence of the divine calling of Jesus Christ than did the Prophet Joseph Smith.

I believe the Prophet Joseph Smith was a prophet because he did many superhuman things. One was translating the Book of Mormon. Some people will not agree, but I submit to you

that the Prophet Joseph Smith in translating the
Book of Mormon did a superhuman work. I ask
you students to undertake to write a story on the
ancient inhabitants of America. Write as he
did without any source of material. Include in
your story fifty-four chapters dealing with
wars, twenty-one historical chapters, fifty-five
chapters on visions and prophecies, and,
remember, when you begin to write on visions
and prophecies you must have your record
agree meticulously with the Bible. You write
seventy-one chapters on doctrine and exhorta-
tion, and, here too, you must check every statement with the scriptures or you will be proven
to be a fraud. You must write twenty-one chapters on the ministry of Christ, and everything
you claim he said and did and every testimony
you write in your book about him must agree
absolutely with the New Testament.

I ask you, would you like to undertake such a

task? I would suggest to you too that you must employ figures of speech, similes, metaphors, narrations, exposition, description, oratory, epic, lyric, logic, and parables. Undertake that, will you? I ask you to remember that the man that translated the Book of Mormon was a young man who hadn't had the opportunity of schooling that you have had, and yet he dictated that book in just a little over two months and made very few, if any, corrections. For over one hundred years, some of the best students and scholars of the world have been trying to prove from the Bible that the Book of Mormon is false, but not one of them has been able to prove that anything he wrote was not in strict harmony with the scriptures, with the Bible, and with the Word of God.

The Book of Mormon not only declares on the title page that its purpose is to convince Jew and Gentile that Jesus is the Christ, the Eternal God, but this truth is the burden of its message. In Third Nephi it is recorded that multitudes of people testified, "We saw him; we felt of his hands and his side; we know he is the Christ."

Joseph Smith undertook and accomplished other superhuman tasks; among them I list the following: He organized the Church. (I call attention to the fact that no constitution effected by human agency has survived one hundred years without modification or amendment, even the Constitution of the United States. The basic law or constitution of the Church has never been altered.) He undertook to carry the gospel message to all nations, which is a superhuman task still in progress. He undertook, by divine command, to gather thousands of people to Zion. He instituted vicarious work for the dead and built temples for that purpose. He promised that certain signs should follow the believers, and there are thousands of witnesses who certify that this promise has been fulfilled.

I said to my friend, "My Lord, I cannot understand your saying to me that my claims are fantastic. Nor can I understand why Christians who claim to believe in Christ would persecute and put to death a man whose whole purpose was to prove the truth of the things they themselves were declaring, namely, that Jesus was the Christ. I could understand them persecuting Joseph if he had said, 'I am Christ,' or if he had said, 'There is no Christ,' or if he had said someone else is Christ; then Christians believing in Christ would be justified in opposing him. But what he said was, 'He whom ye claim to serve, declare I unto you.' Paraphrasing what Paul said in Athens, 'Whom therefore ye ignorantly worship, him declare I unto you' (Acts 17:23). Joseph said to the Christians of his day, 'You claim to believe in Jesus Christ. I testify that I saw him and I talked with him. He is the Son of God. Why persecute me for that?'

"When Joseph came out of the woods he had at least four fundamental truths, and he announced them to the world. First, that the Father and the Son are separate and distinct individuals. Secondly, that the canon of scripture is not complete. Thirdly, that man was created in the bodily image of God. And fourth, the channel between earth and heaven is open and revelation is continuous."

Perhaps some of you are wondering how the judge reacted to our discussion. He sat and listened intently; he asked some very pointed and searching questions and at the end of the period he said, "Mr. Brown, I wonder if your people appreciate the import of your message; do you?" He said, "If what you have told me is true, it is the greatest message that has come to this earth since the angels announced the birth of Christ."

This was a judge speaking, a great statesman, an intelligent man. He threw out the challenge, "Do you appreciate the import of what you say?" He added: "I wish it were true. I hope it may be true. God knows it ought to be true. I would to God," he said, and he wept as he said it, "that some man could appear on earth and authoritatively say, 'Thus saith the Lord.'"

As I intimated, we did not meet again. I have brought to you very briefly some of the reasons why I believe that Joseph Smith was a prophet of God. But undergirding and overarching all that, I say to you from the very center of my heart that by the revelations of the Holy Ghost I know that Joseph Smith was a prophet of God. While these evidences and many others that could be cited may have the effect of giving one an intellectual conviction, only by the whisperings of the Holy Spirit can one come to know the things of God. By those whisperings, I say I

know that Joseph Smith is a prophet of God. I
thank God for that knowledge and pray for his
blessings upon all of you in the name of Jesus
Christ, amen.

From a transcript of an address given at Brigham Young
University on 4 October 1955, while Elder Brown was serving as
Assistant to the Twelve.